WRITING MEANINGFUL
TEACHER EVALUATIONS
—RIGHT NOW!!

CORWIN
PRESS

The Corwin Press logo—a raven striding across an open book—represents the happy union of courage and learning. We are a professional-level publisher of books and journals for K–12 educators, and we are committed to creating and providing resources that embody these qualities. Corwin's motto is "Success for All Learners."

WRITING MEANINGFUL
TEACHER EVALUATIONS
—RIGHT NOW!!

The

Principal's

Quick-Start

Reference

Guide

Cornelius L. Barker
Claudette J. Searchwell

CORWIN PRESS, INC.
A Sage Publications Company
Thousand Oaks, California

For information address:

Corwin Press, Inc.
A Sage Publications Company
2455 Teller Road
Thousand Oaks, California 91320
E-mail: order@corwinpress.com

SAGE Publications Ltd.
6 Bonhill Street
London EC2A 4PU
United Kingdom

SAGE Publications India Pvt. Ltd.
M-32 Market
Greater Kailash I
New Delhi 110 048 India

Printed in the United States of America

Library of Congress Cataloging-in-Publication Data

Barker, Cornelius L.
    Writing meaningful teacher evaluations—right now!! : The principal's quick-start reference guide / by Cornelius L. Barker and Claudette J. Searchwell.
        p. cm.
    ISBN 0-8039-6732-2 (cloth : acid-free paper)
    ISBN 0-8039-6733-0 (pbk. : acid-free paper)
    1. Teachers—Rating of—United States—Handbooks, manuals, etc.
    2. Performance standards—United States—Handbooks, manuals, etc.
    I. Searchwell, Claudette J. II. Title.
    LB2838 .B293 1998
    371.14'4—ddc21   98-9080

This book is printed on acid-free paper.

    99 00 01 02 03 04 10 9 8 7 6 5 4 3 2

Production Editor: Sherrise M. Purdum
Editorial Assistant: Kristen L. Gibson
Editorial Assistant: Nevair Kabakian
Typesetter/Designer: Marion Warren
Cover Designer: Michele Lee

CONTENTS

FOREWORD

This manual is treasured by those who own it. As a professor of education for 30 years, I have reviewed dozens of teacher evaluation guides. This is in a category of its own. No other guide includes the "benchmarks" of effective teaching in the manner of *Writing Meaningful Teacher Evaluations—Right Now!!*

It has been my pleasure to share it with colleagues at Seton Hall University College of Education and Human Services and then have to beg for its return. The obvious use is for supervisors and administrators who are required to perform evaluations of teaching. Its organization of classroom and teaching characteristics is complete and thorough. I cannot think of any area of classroom climate or instructional descriptor that has been omitted. The manner in which the guide is organized for an administrator or supervisor of instruction makes the process of writing evaluations a less than tedious task. It actually makes it a pleasant task. And, what is more, it makes the achievement of more effective teaching reachable with its suggestions for improvement.

Another use is for university courses in supervision for the reasons outlined in the former paragraph. I can envision the use of videotaped teaching episodes for such classes, in which graduate students would perform evaluations using this guide.

I found a novel use for the manual in my Seminar in Student Teaching with senior students. The guide is used as criteria for effective teaching. Students perform in-class demonstrations of the characteristics outlined. Students also use it for self-evaluations of their own student teaching performance.

There is much that can be recommended; creative professors and supervisors of instruction will find a myriad of ways to use this guide. The more I use it, the more ways I find for its applications. Curriculum, instruction, classroom climate, enhancement of self-esteem, and organizing for teaching are readily evaluated by the use of the manual. Its applications will continue for as long as the process of education in classrooms everywhere continues. It is current and has a bright future.

ANGELA M. RAIMO, Ed.D., J.D.
Professor of Education and Education Law
Seton Hall University, South Orange, New Jersey

PREFACE

Writing Meaningful Teacher Evaluations—Right Now!! was designed with the busy administrator/supervisor in mind!

The evaluation of staff performance, being fundamental to the viability of the school program, is one of the more thought-provoking and time-consuming duties performed by an administrator, supervisor, or department chairperson.

Now there is a better way to accomplish this task—quickly and easily—without compromising the integrity of the written assessment.

Even the most subtle nuance of teaching performance can be captured when using the Guide as a foundation on which classroom observations/evaluations are built.

Certainly those new to the field of administration will find the Guide invaluable . . . and experienced administrators, who occasionally search for a particular word or phrase, might seek assistance from the array of suggested statements it contains.

Whatever form a district uses for its evaluation instrument, the Guide is suitable for use with that form! From the comment/suggestion section of a checklist format to a narrative format, *Writing Meaningful Teacher Evaluations—Right Now!!* will make writing comprehensive evaluations easier.

Part I

Five standard performance areas list benchmark skills relevant to what is universally associated with sound teaching skills:

1. Proficiency With Curriculum

   This section outlines teacher performance and provides elements that answer the question "Did the teacher exhibit a strong knowledge base and deliver instruction in a way that maximized student understanding and retention of skills and information?"

2. Evaluating Student Growth

The statements in this area answer the questions "Does the teacher implement strategies that promote student achievement?" and "Is student progress monitored, assessed, and remediated, when needed?"

3. Preparation and Readiness

This section seeks to determine "Does the teacher plan comprehensively and use materials that motivate students to participate and gain insight?" "Are sound personal and professional attributes evidenced?"

4. Instructional Performance

This section allows the evaluator to gauge the quality of instructional delivery. It seeks to answer the question "Does the teacher practice techniques that are professionally sound and that result in measurable student achievement?"

5. Interaction/Climate

This section asks the question "Is a learning environment maintained in which each student is valued for his or her unique contributions?" "As a result of the teacher's efforts, are students thriving in an atmosphere that promotes well-being and achievement?"

Part 1 also includes sections titled "Vocabulary Aids" and sections in which statements geared to applaud excellent performance are offered under the name of "Suggested 'Pats on the Back.'"

Part 2

Using experiences culled from more than 50 combined years in education and through observing standard practices used in evaluating the delivery of instruction, as well as attendance at conferences/workshops and through extensive readings, the authors determined it would be helpful to address the issues presented in Part 2.

Here, the user of the Guide is offered practical assistance with many of the ancillary areas that present themselves to the administrator-supervisor when evaluating staff.

In "Common Areas of Concern, With Suggested Remedies," basic remedial actions are listed for some of the more common teaching deficiencies encountered.

The "Evaluation Organizer," an innovative tool on which observed classroom practices can be noted, allows the busy administrator/supervisor to easily transcribe brief notations into in-depth statements.

Read the "Sample Written Evaluations" and their commentary to see if you have not encountered similar situations in your evaluation efforts.

In them you will be able to see how even subtle nuances of teaching performance can be captured.

The "Cross-Reference of Key Terms" section will help you quickly find needed statements by using key words and phrases.

"Chronology of Evaluation Activities" is offered as a sample of the steps that can be taken throughout the school year in light of your tenured/nontenured, excellent or marginal staff.

Duplicate the page entitled "Record of Evaluations" and keep a running record of your progress as you complete informal observations and formal evaluations with exit conferences.

Duplicate the "Checklist of Basic Documentation and/or Conditions" and take a copy with you as you visit instructional areas on both informal and formal evaluation occasions.

Use *Writing Meaningful Teacher Evaluations—Right Now!!* in any way that suits your particular needs for writing evaluations that are always comprehensive—and on time!!

CLAUDETTE J. SEARCHWELL

ABOUT THE AUTHORS

Cornelius L. Barker is a much sought-after lecturer for school and community groups on the subject of current cognitive and behavioral trends exhibited by today's youth. His career in education has spanned more than 25 years in the capacity of classroom teacher and administrator on both the elementary and secondary levels.

He is currently serving as a building administrator in a large secondary school.

Claudette J. Searchwell is a retired elementary school principal whose career spanned 34 years in the public schools. Her service in the field of education included posts as classroom teacher, assistant director of a federal basic skills program, coordinator of citywide after-school and summer programs, assistant principal, and principal.

She is now a member of the adjunct staff at Kean University, Union, New Jersey, serving as supervisor of pre-certification students completing their senior internship.

INTRODUCTION

Why Is This Guide Needed?

Evaluating school personnel occupies a core position among the many practices that are geared toward ensuring quality performance in our classrooms.

Just as student performance is routinely assessed, so must the skills of those responsible for educating children be monitored, supported, and facilitated.

The expertise required of those who assess the quality of the delivery of instruction is immense. Teachers expect, and are entitled, to receive evaluations that are specific and geared toward recognizing excellence—or the need for improvement—where it exists.

There are many tools available to support the efforts of administrators in the performance of their tasks. Why not a tool to promote easier manageability when completing written evaluations? To an ever-increasing degree, pivotal decisions concerning the future of education will rest on the skills of those delivering instruction—as well as on those empowered to monitor their performance.

This Guide will assist administrators in consistently producing evaluations for each of their teachers—with a minimum of time invested.

What a Good Written Evaluation Looks Like

Here are two examples of written evaluations. The first has been completed without using the Guide. Notice that it is lacking specific reference to the activities witnessed during the lesson and fails to relate the rich and unique quality of the teacher's presentation. **It could be anyone's evaluation!**

The second was completed using the Guide as an administrative tool.

INDEPENDENT SCHOOL DISTRICT
Staff Evaluation

EMPLOYEE: Ms. Paula Denson   **SCHOOL:** Main High School

ASSIGNMENT: Mathematics   **DATE:**   0/0/00

OBJECTIVE: To comprehend mathematical operations involved in calculating the third angle of a triangle.

Independent group activity: Review of test taken on parallel lines.

A. KNOWLEDGE OF SUBJECT MATTER   __S__   D. QUALITY OF INSTRUCTION   __S__

B. MEASURE OF STUDENT GROWTH   __S__   E. LEARNING ENVIRONMENT   __S__

C. DESIGN AND STRUCTURE   __S__

Students on roll: 30   Present: 23
Homework: Read pp. 105, 106; complete p. 106, exer. 1-10.

A. KNOWLEDGE OF SUBJECT MATTER:

Knows curriculum.
Test reviewed. Math definitions given.
Used resource materials and A-V.
Students interested.

B. MEASURE OF STUDENT GROWTH:

Homework assigned.
All students will learn.
Rewards all students for trying.
Ms. D answers students' questions.

C. DESIGN AND STRUCTURE:

Good classroom behavior.
Used guide. Had instructional objective.
Good planbook and rollbook.
Excellent activities.

D. QUALITY OF INSTRUCTION:

Gives students time to answer.
She tells what is expected of students.
Maximizes time on task.

E. QUALITY OF LEARNING ENVIRONMENT:

Room quiet and neat.
Sets high expectations.
Respects students.
Keeps attention of all students.

SUMMARY: This was a very good lesson. Ms. D is a fine teacher.

INDEPENDENT SCHOOL DISTRICT
Staff Evaluation

EMPLOYEE: Ms. Paula Denson   **SCHOOL:** Main High School

ASSIGNMENT: Mathematics   **DATE:** 0/0/00

OBJECTIVE: To comprehend mathematical operations involved in calculating the third angle of a triangle.

Independent group activity: Review of test taken on parallel lines.

A. KNOWLEDGE OF SUBJECT MATTER	S	D. QUALITY OF INSTRUCTION	S
B. MEASURE OF STUDENT GROWTH	S	E. LEARNING ENVIRONMENT	S
C. DESIGN AND STRUCTURE	S		

Students on roll: 30   Present: 23
Homework: Read pp. 105, 106; complete p. 106, exer. 1-10.

A. KNOWLEDGE OF SUBJECT MATTER:

Ms. D *demonstrates a comprehensive knowledge of the subject area* of math in her use of the textbook (Chapter 3—"Calculating Angles"). She *displays a clear understanding of the subject matter,* which she displayed throughout her delivery of the lesson.

Ms. D *began the lesson with the dissemination of review material from previously acquired skills,* which included work on the identification of the presence of parallel lines in diagrams. Ample opportunities were provided for the students to define the problems to be addressed after she *provided for the definition of the concepts and the description of skills* necessary for solving the problems on the chalkboard.

She *provided review materials containing activities related to future learning,* with special emphasis placed on the review of theorems 17-19.

Ms. D *demonstrated an awareness of how children learn through the use of developmentally appropriate hands-on material* in the form of self-help worksheets.

Ms. D *provided opportunities for the application of acquired knowledge* by allowing the students to practice calculating the third angle of a triangle as a part of their seatwork.

The materials used were highly appropriate and contributed to the overall clarity of the lesson.

B. MEASURE OF STUDENT GROWTH:

All students were given an equal opportunity to contribute when a three-part quiz sheet was distributed during the classroom session. Ms. D was able to *accurately measure the degree to which student comprehension met the objective of the lesson* through this quiz and other work aids.

The *students were given the opportunity to interact with one another in testing their newly acquired skills* by working in groups to solve problems. The *students were encouraged to share their conclusions in a climate of acceptance and dignity.*

All were aided as Ms. D *circulated among the students, providing assistance.* It was explained to the students that the homework assignment would count as a part of their grade in determining the degree of mastery regarding the identification of, and proving the presence of, parallel lines in a triangle.

Ms. D *invited questions and encouraged the students to challenge any concept* regarding the lesson before leaving class for the day.

C. DESIGN AND STRUCTURE:

The students settled into the activities immediately after entering the classroom and began work with *materials that were well chosen for students with varied learning styles.* A review of the planbook revealed that *alternate plans were provided for students of varied competencies.*

Ms. D explained that she intended to *use A-V (overhead projector) to enhance the quality of the lesson and to support her students' understanding of the lesson being presented.*

It was noted that the curriculum guide remained visible on the desk throughout the lesson. A review of the planbook showed that Ms. D *uses the curriculum guide to plan detailed lesson plans.*

Ms. D *maintains a legible and comprehensive rollbook.*

It must be noted that Ms. D *demonstrated competence and ease during the evaluation session,* which can be attributed to her high degree of preparedness.

D. QUALITY OF INSTRUCTION:

Throughout the observed classroom session, Ms. D implemented effective instructional techniques, *providing optimum learning experiences for her students.* She *encouraged her students to think and to problem solve.* Ms. D *engaged the students in activities geared toward enhancing their critical thinking skills,* such as the questions posed regarding the mathematical strategies that could be used in solving the problems of the day. It must be noted that *ample "wait time" was provided to encourage all learners to participate.* This strategy was *employed to gain attention and to maintain focus on the lesson.*

Ms. D's method of teaching *stimulated student participation through the use of covert techniques of providing information,* as demonstrated by placing answers on the board and requiring the students to match them with the correct problems, much in the manner of a *Jeopardy* game activity.

Ms. D's *lesson was innovative and clearly motivated the students to want to learn.*

E. QUALITY OF LEARNING ENVIRONMENT:

It is clear that Ms. D *respects individual differences in the learning styles of the students without compromising classroom objectives.* She *maintains high expectations and communicates them clearly to all students.*

Ms. D *created and used effective behavior modification through* her appointment of consensus ideas to a cooperative group spokesperson, who then verbalized group consensus ideas to the class.

SUMMARY: Ms. D adeptly led the students through the discovery process and on to a logical conclusion. Progress in meeting the stated objectives of the lesson was evident. It was evident that a great deal of planning and preparation went into the lesson. The best of sound professional practices have been exhibited during this lesson. Ms. D is a great asset to Main High School. Keep up the good work!

Which of these two examples meets the standard for quality written evaluations that you want for your teachers?

Part I

WRITING THE EVALUATION

Performance Statements, Vocabulary Aids, and Suggested "Pats on the Back"

This section contains

- Proficiency With Curriculum
- Evaluating Student Growth
- Preparation and Readiness
- Instructional Performance
- Interaction/Climate

Section I

PROFICIENCY WITH CURRICULUM

This section assists the administrator/supervisor in determining if a sound knowledge base of core curriculum standards and district/school curriculum mandates have been demonstrated.

Performance statements in this section include

A. Anticipatory Set
B. Clarity of Presentation
C. Student Motivation
D. Professional Ability
E. Professional Strategies
F. Promoting Student Understanding
G. Closure

Performance Statements

A. Anticipatory Set

1. Relates lesson content to child's feelings and experiences in order to personally involve students in the learning.

2. Clearly explains the lesson objectives and learning tasks.

3. Provides for definition of concepts and description of skills.

4. Relates lesson content to prior and/or future learning.

5. Communicates directions and models the required activities, when needed.

6. Begins class with material related to the prior lesson/s, providing students with transfer information to establish the basis for them to learn (understand) the new skill/s (concept/s, etc.).

7. Uses personal experiences to afford students a realistic approach to the concept.

8. Begins instruction with a synopsis of the instructional objective and its correlation to the lesson's objective.

9. Communicates expectations for learning.

10. Employs opening activities that are purposeful and geared toward establishing a concrete framework for presentation of new skills.

B. Clarity of Presentation

1. Enhances understanding through use of appropriate resource and/or supplemental materials.

2. Stresses important points and dimensions of concepts.

3. Presents information in an appropriate sequence.

4. Provides opportunities for application of acquired skills.

5. Provides for elaboration of critical aspect of concepts.

6. Designs activities congruent to the objectives of the lesson.

7. Enhances the students' understanding of the concept/s (lesson/s, skill/s, etc.) through the use of A-V materials.

8. Provides a sequential array of learning activities, ensuring that the desired goals are reached.

9. Presents facts of the lesson accurately and in sequence.

10. Reflects the objective of the lesson while conducting lesson activities.

C. Student Motivation

1. Uses strategies geared toward motivating students in the learning process.

2. Uses strategies to motivate students to learn.

3. Provides opportunities for students to experience the processes of discovery and creativity.

4. Challenges students to understand the process by which answers are reached.

5. Makes relevant to the experiences of the students all aspects of the learning situation.

6. Relates the relevancy of an education to the students.

7. Displays a clear understanding of the subject matter.

8. Uses knowledge of subject matter (curriculum, textbook, subject) to enhance presentation with supplemental information (materials, etc.).

9. Involves students in the art (skill) of discovery through (describe activity).

10. Instills a desire to learn in the students.

D. Professional Ability

1. Demonstrates knowledge of subject matter through involvement in professional presentations (written work, speeches, etc.).

2. Provides evidence of participating in professional development activities (workshops, seminars, conventions, continuing education courses, etc.).

3. Combines textbook knowledge with practical life experiences when presenting concepts.

4. Demonstrates a high level of professionalism in the performance of duties.

5. Avoids reliance on commercially prepared materials (curriculum, etc.) that focus on narrowly defined academic skills.

6. Provides literature-based instruction, making connections to other subjects.

7. Provides whole language method of instruction, integrating reading, writing, thinking, listening, viewing, and speaking skills.

8. Demonstrates skill in written (oral) communication.

9. Provides review material/s containing activities related to future learning.

10. Demonstrates highly professional writing (speaking) skills.

E. Professional Strategies

1. Elicits critical thinking skills to assess students' comprehension of subject matter.

2. Poses questions at various levels of comprehension.

3. Assists students in the development of critical thinking skills (name other skills) to access information.

4. Uses activities leading to (or enhancing) the cognitive development of the students (group, class).

5. Employs strategies geared toward enhancing students' intellectual abilities and problem-solving skills.

6. Uses activities (materials) appropriate to the varied learning styles within the group.

7. Provides for teacher-integrated (blended) subject areas (disciplines).

8. Maintains focus by teaching to the objectives.

9. Integrates subject matter with the infusion of varied skills.

10. Demonstrates an awareness of how children learn through the use of developmentally appropriate hands-on material/s.

F. Promoting Student Understanding

1. Teaches at appropriate level of difficulty after assessing needs (abilities) of students.

2. Selects appropriate level of difficulty when writing objectives (plans).

3. Poses thought-provoking questions.

4. Assists students in gaining (maintaining) sound writing skills through emphasis on punctuation (grammar, spelling, sentence structure, syntax, etc.).

5. Assists students in gaining (maintaining) sound communication skills through emphasis on grammar (vocabulary, listening skills, etc.).

6. Establishes learning centers.

7. Displays visuals that are relevant to the objective/s.

8. Reteaches concept/s, when required.

9. Maintains appropriate pacing, reflective of the students' best interest.

10. Provides information that is correct and trains students in technique/s of finding, analyzing, and utilizing information.

G. Closure

1. Gives students opportunities to cement their acquired knowledge through participation in creative activities, such as playwriting (creative writing, oral reports, etc.).

2. Allows students to demonstrate enthusiasm for subject matter, through their participation in the activities.

3. Provides a forum for sharing students' conclusions in a climate of acceptance and dignity.

4. Provides opportunities for the application of acquired knowledge.

5. Assists and challenges students to become self-directed learners.

6. Summarizes learning and allows students sufficient time to internalize the material (concepts, etc.).

7. Allows sufficient time to explain homework and to provide closure to the day's activities.

8. Ends the lesson with a review and dissemination of materials related to the skills, for home study.

9. Checks for understanding before distributing written assignments.

10. Assigns independent seatwork (homework) relevant to the lesson.

Vocabulary Aids

This section has been supplied to assist you with the optional rewriting of any of the suggested statements found in the Guide. Searching for that one word that best expresses the thought you wish to convey? Use the Vocabulary Aids section and put that word right at your fingertips!!

academic	expertise	orientation
accomplished	familiar with	originate
accurate	grasp of	pedagogy
acumen	inadequate	pedantic
adept	indepthful	poor
adequate	ingenious	precise
adroit	innovative	proficient
astute	intellectual	profound
aware	intelligent	sage
awesome	inventive	scant knowledge of
brainy	keen	scholarly
bright	know-how	scope of knowledge
clear	knowledgeable	shallow
clever	learned	skilled
comprehensive	lucid	strong
creative	marginal	substantive
dedicated	masterful	talented
developed	mastery	understands
diligent	mediocre	varied
endowed	minimal knowledge of	wisdom
erudite	multifaceted	

Suggested "Pats on the Back"

This section is geared to provide you with ideas for choosing just the right words to applaud exemplary performance. We hope you will have cause to make liberal use of Suggested "Pats on the Back."

A. You made the lesson "come alive" for the students.

B. Your command of the content area/s (course guide, curriculum, material, chapter, etc.) was demonstrated through your fact-filled presentation.

C. The lesson was made more interesting through the use of the supplemental material supplied to the class.

D. Your creative use of real-life examples gave the students an excellent insight into the main concept/s of the lesson.

E. Your opening (exercises, demonstration, statements, etc.) captured the interest of the class.

F. Your presentation was cogent and concise.

G. The students were clearly motivated to participate in your class.

H. The use of (state type of A-V material used) enhanced student understanding of the lesson content.

I. The materials used were highly appropriate and contributed to the overall clarity of the lesson.

J. The lesson clearly met the stated instructional objective/s.

K. Your active involvement in the activities supported and motivated the students to achieve.

L. It was apparent that the students benefited from your timely feedback and discussion.

M. You adeptly led the students through the discovery process on to a logical conclusion.

N. Students demonstrated that they had a clear understanding of the concept/s (skills, information, procedures, etc.) being presented.

O. Your follow-up exercises were highly appropriate and useful in cementing students' newly acquired skills.

Section 2

EVALUATING STUDENT GROWTH

This section assists the administrator/supervisor in determining whether the observed instructional practices promote student academic achievement.

Performance statements in this section include

A. Techniques Aiding Comprehension
B. Monitoring Activities
C. Goal-Setting Strategies
D. Empowering Students to Succeed
E. Employing Current Strategies to Evaluate Students
F. Evaluation

Performance Statements

A. Techniques Aiding Comprehension

1. Provides students feedback and possible resolution/s to their problems (concerns, etc.).

2. Provides timely and constructive feedback.

3. Provides for demonstration of examples of skill/s on the chalkboard prior to the students being asked to demonstrate proficiency.

4. Provides forum for students to address the problem/s in a variety of ways.

5. Provides ongoing feedback to maintain the students' focus.

6. Varies instructional technique to accommodate the varied learning styles of the group.

7. Assesses whether each student is achieving expected goal/s and adjusts the activity accordingly.

8. Designs plan to aid students in problem solving such as (describe project).

9. Invites questions and encourages students to challenge concepts (statements, theories, etc.).

10. Routinely incorporates test-taking skills into the lesson in order to familiarize students with the mechanics of taking tests (examinations).

B. Monitoring Activities

1. Conducts ongoing check/s for comprehension.
2. Monitors students' written work and provides positive feedback.
3. Monitors students' work and provides timely feedback.
4. Checks for comprehension, using a variety of methods.
5. Provides individual (group) assistance on an ongoing basis.
6. Monitors students' progress during independent practice.
7. Corrects incorrect responses with patience (dignity).
8. Involves students in the art of reinforcing knowledge and skills through (describe activity).
9. Circulates among students, providing assistance.
10. Assesses student behavior/s relevant to the learning environment.

C. Goal-Setting Strategies

1. Allows for (encourages) students to plan expected accomplishments prior to commencing project (lesson) activities.
2. Clearly defines the expectations for satisfying course (lesson) requirements.
3. Sets high expectations and provides ample opportunities for growth.
4. Communicates a belief in the potential of all students.
5. Shares authority and responsibility for positive learning outcomes with students (parents, community groups, etc.).
6. Allows for pupil goal-setting and self-evaluation.
7. Promotes enthusiasm for subject matter to promote student learning.
8. Motivates students to learn through the extensive interest (talent, information, experiences, etc.) brought to the subject.
9. Inspires students through creative (hands-on, interdisciplinary, experiential, etc.) method/s of presentation of subject matter.
10. Allows students to reach conclusions using a variety of methods.

D. Empowering Students to Succeed

1. Acknowledges efforts of students of varied competencies.

2. Establishes classroom policies for student accountability.

3. Displays student work that is reflective of their progress.

4. Displays knowledge of individual students' motivation and uses this knowledge to support progress and greater achievement/s.

5. Provides an opportunity for students to interact with one another in testing their newly acquired skills.

6. Guides (assists) students to realize (articulate, visualize, actualize) short- and/or long-term goals.

7. Gives students ample opportunity to demonstrate mastery.

8. Maintains high expectations for students.

9. Guides students toward academic independence through (describe activity).

10. Encourages students to think and problem solve.

E. Employing Current Strategies to Evaluate Students

1. Utilizes current technology to clarify and enhance learning.

2. Encourages and facilitates students' recognition and understanding of learning as a process through (describe activity).

3. Motivates students to reach (exceed) goals through (describe technique/s).

4. Assesses students' ability to comprehend learning as a process.

5. Motivates students to excel through innovative (describe technique/s).

6. Adopts a system of performance-based education in which creative assessment is key.

7. Allows for student ability to be measured by giving them the opportunity to demonstrate mastery through (describe activity).

8. Provides for tests (quizzes) that reflect the lesson objective/s.

9. Checks individual students (groups) for understanding through questioning and observation.

10. Maintains a comprehensive record of student progress.

F. Evaluation

1. Tests for comprehension in both traditional and nontraditional ways, such as integrated studies projects, problem solving,

videotape review, multimedia presentations, alternative grading system, and so on.

2. Monitors students' portfolios and uses assessment data as a tool to promote student academic growth.

3. Uses classwork and/or homework assignments to assess comprehension of the subject matter.

4. Familiarizes the students with the mechanics of test-taking through the use of exercises that employ test-taking skills.

5. Accurately measures the degree to which student learning (comprehension) meets the objective/s of the lesson.

6. Uses teacher-made (criterion-referenced, achievement) tests to determine mastery.

7. Using the rollbook, shows evidence of formal (informal) evaluations.

8. Conducts frequent monitoring of students' progress via quizzes (tests, homework, etc.).

9. Elicits overt written (signalling, choral) behaviors to verify student learning.

10. Encourages students to conduct varied self-evaluation strategies, including checklists, editing, portfolios, and journals.

Vocabulary Aids

This section has been supplied to assist you with the optional rewriting of any of the suggested statements found in the Guide. Searching for that one word that best expresses the thought you wish to convey? Use the Vocabulary Aids section and put that word right at your fingertips!!

abusive	disparage	modeling
accelerate	effort	motivate
accountability	enhance	nonjudgmental
accountable	equity	nonpartisan
adaptable	estimate	observant
advocate	estimation	observe
alert	evaluate	open
analysis	explain	opinion
analyze	expound	opinionated
appraise	fair	organized
appreciate	flexible	outcome
approval	genuine	overt
articulate	grace period	painstaking
assess	growth	participant
assure	guarded	perceive

attentive	guide	perception
awareness	hardworking	precise
beneficial	helpful	preliminary
biased	honesty	preparation
bolster	impartiality	progress
censure	improvement	proponent
checked	increase	reasonable
comprehensive	incremental	receptive
concerned	insensitive	reliable
condemn	integrity	reproach
confirm	interested in	responsible
conscientious	interpret	results
considerate	involvement	sagacity
contribute	judgment	show interest in
covert	judgmental	sincere
credible	judicious	skillful
denounce	just	stimulate
dialogue	justice	strengthen
diminished	knowledge	supervise
diplomacy	lenient	supportive
direct	levelheaded	tendency
directions	liable	treatment
discern	mastery	unfair
discreet	maximize	unhelpful
discretion	method	unreliable
discriminate	methodology	varied
discussion	mindful	viewpoint

Suggested "Pats on the Back"

This section is geared to provide you with ideas for choosing just the right words to applaud exemplary performance. We hope you will have cause to make liberal use of Suggested "Pats on the Back."

A. The class activities support stated goals of skill mastery of (course guide, curriculum, specific name of test, etc.).

B. Progress is evident in meeting stated objective/s of (lesson, specific name of test, annual performance projection, etc.).

C. Students profit from your keen insight into their individual strengths and weaknesses.

D. Students were given excellent and timely feedback regarding their (written work, homework, questions, concerns, projects, etc.).

E. Your ability to maintain an excellent record of student progress was demonstrated through the in-depth (improvement plans, marking book, student folders, portfolios, journal notations, etc.) that you provided.

F. The (posters, charts, papers, bulletin boards, etc.) were aesthetically arranged and relevant to the subject matter (unit of work) being taught.

G. The (learning center/s, bulletin boards, posters, charts, etc.) served to enhance student understanding and learning.

H. Students profited from the individualized attention shown to them.

I. You demonstrated skill in supporting and motivating your students to learn (succeed, work, participate, strive for excellence, etc.).

J. You set attainable goals for your students and motivated them to reach and exceed them.

K. Students appeared eager, motivated, and happy in your classroom.

L. You skillfully led your students through the processes of (discovery, inferential comprehension, critical thinking, experiential learning, etc.) through (describe activity).

M. You are to be commended on the excellent and timely manner in which you evaluate, record, and return students' written work.

N. You are to be commended on the wide variety of supplemental activities you prepared for the class.

O. You demonstrated creativity and skill in your method/s of assessing comprehension of the lesson.

Section 3 ✎

PREPARATION AND READINESS

This section assists the administrator/supervisor in determining the impact of the quality of planning and the degree of organization on the observed lesson. In addition, practices related to professional performance are addressed.

Performance statements in this section include

A. Planbook/Record Keeping
B. Materials
C. Professional Preparation

Performance Statements

A. Planbook/Record Keeping

1. The planbook was comprehensive and up-to-date.

2. A review of the planbook shows evidence of preparation of a variety of practical learning experiences for the students.

3. Designs innovative lessons using current events (manipulatives, A-V, demonstrations, etc.) to stimulate learning.

4. Plans a variety of activities (questions, discussion, written practice) to promote understanding.

5. Uses an interdisciplinary approach to (teaching, planning, etc.)

6. Records teaching adjustments in the planbook.

7. Maintains records that are accurate, thorough, and up-to-date.

8. Can articulate students' progress to parents (students, specialists).

9. By using alternate plans, provides for students of varied competencies.

10. Selects appropriate level of difficulty when writing objectives (lesson plans, activities, etc.).

B. Materials

1. Displays teacher-made visual aids (posters, bulletin boards, etc.) to complement and support current curriculum activities.

2. Displays students' work that is reflective of their progress.

3. Supplements reading materials with library/collection of student high-interest books (pamphlets, etc.).

4. Supplies materials geared to promote hands-on experiences that support curriculum activities.

5. Uses A-V to enhance quality of lesson and support student comprehension (understanding) of the lesson (skills, task, etc.) being presented.

6. Provides well-chosen and effective materials for working with students with varied learning styles.

7. Selects activities that support lesson objectives.

8. Makes a wide variety of teacher-made materials available.

9. Prepares teaching aids relevant to the objectives.

10. Provides and maintains relevant reinforcement materials.

C. Professional Preparation

1. Anticipates potential problems and implements strategies to avoid (diminish, alter, etc.) negative consequences.

2. Strives to solve problems through the use of professional training and expertise to preserve student welfare and maintain a climate for learning.

3. Demonstrates mature response to constructive criticism (suggestions) and seeks to effect a positive change in the area/s under discussion.

4. Maintains a highly professional appearance (manner).

5. Maintains an excellent record of attendance.

6. Is dependable and consistent in reporting to school (duty assignments, meetings, etc.) on time.

7. Demonstrates a high level of preparedness and competence in terms of planning (completing written reports/records, etc.).

8. Demonstrates competence and ease during observation/evaluation sessions.

9. Plans comprehensively.

10. Plans lesson objectives around developmental needs and/or interests of the students.

Vocabulary Aids

This section has been supplied to assist you with the optional rewriting of any of the suggested statements found in the Guide. Searching for that one word that best expresses the thought you wish to convey? Use the Vocabulary Aids section and put that word right at your fingertips!!

aesthetic	faithful	precision
alert to	find fault (with)	preparedness
arrange	force	reaction
artistic	grace	refine
assignment	guide	reliable
assortment	heed	repercussion
attention	improve	reproach
authoritative	increase	responsible
avail self of	instruction	restrain
barren	introduction	review
behavior	justify	rule
benefit from	leadership	show interest in
berate	lesson	skillful
calm	manage	stable
care	management	steadfast
careful	mannerly	sterile
chaotic	maximize	strong
clarity	objective	style
clean	opinion	supervise
command	order	supplements
composure	orderly	supplies
concern	organization	system
conduct	organized	take charge of
confidence	orientation	task
control	oversee	tendency toward
demonstration	partake in	tidy
deportment	passive	timely
design	pattern of	unprepared
directions	performance	untenable
discipline	permissive	untidy
disorderly	perseverance	unusual
disparage	perturbed	vigilant
document	plans	waste
dominate	polite	watchful
duty	positive	weak
equity	precise	well-groomed
		well-prepared

Suggested "Pats on the Back"

This section is geared to provide you with ideas for choosing just the right words to applaud exemplary performance. We hope you will have cause to make liberal use of Suggested "Pats on the Back."

A. Your planbook (and/or rollbook) reflects excellent planning and record-keeping. A highly professional job!

B. Your plans reflect that you are following the prescribed (course guide, curriculum, grade level syllabus, etc.).

C. (Teacher's name) maintains a highly professional appearance and demeanor.

D. It is evident that a great deal of planning and preparation went into your lesson. Good work!

E. You model excellent (writing, speaking, professional, etc.) skills for your students.

F. (Teacher's name) is committed to providing learning experiences of high quality, as evidenced by the planning/preparedness for the class.

G. The use of (specify A-V) enhanced understanding of the lesson content.

H. All the records relevant to tracking the progress of your students have been found to be highly comprehensive and professionally done.

I. Your plans reflect your child-centered focus. You are to be commended!

J. The posters (charts, bulletin boards, etc.) are aesthetic and relevant to the subject matter (unit of work, etc.) being taught.

K. You are to be complimented on the wide variety of supplemental activities (materials) you prepared for this lesson.

L. Your planning reflects your keen awareness of current educational trends.

M. (Teacher's name) reflects the highest standards of professionalism in the performance of all teaching duties. He/She is to be commended!

N. (Teacher's name) is receptive to administrative suggestions and works well within the framework of all professional (district, school) mandates.

O. Your students benefit from the professional maturity you bring to the classroom, which is evident from your preparation and the delivery of the lesson.

Section 4

INSTRUCTIONAL PERFORMANCE

This section assists the administrator/supervisor in assessing the quality of instructional delivery witnessed during the observed lesson. These practices are also viewed in terms of their positive effect on students.

Performance statements in this section include

A. Teaching Style
B. Promoting Student Academic Growth
C. Educational Practices

Performance Statements

A. Teaching Style

1. Varies instructional style in accordance with student needs.
2. Employs the lecture (question-answer, modeling, chalk-talk) method of instruction.
3. Delivers lesson in a manner geared to support students' success using modulated tones (animation, creativity, eye appeal, dramatic gestures, etc.).
4. Employs strategies to gain attention and maintain focus on the lesson.
5. Employs teacher-directed activities using textbooks, drill, practice, worksheets, group instruction, etc.
6. Maximizes time-on-task.
7. Provides ample "wait time" in order to encourage all learners to participate.
8. Commands the attention and cooperation of all students in the class.
9. Correlates goal-setting with the level of difficulty.
10. Consistently provides equity to all students in terms of opportunity to participate in classroom activities.

B. Promoting Student Academic Growth

1. Encourages students to remain focused on the lesson.

2. Clearly communicates learning expectations.

3. Uses questioning strategies geared to all ability levels.

4. Engages students in activities geared toward enhancing their critical thinking skills.

5. Closely monitors students' work and adjusts teaching when needed.

6. Utilizes school facilities (resource personnel, etc.) to the maximum benefit of the students.

7. Implements effective instructional techniques that provide optimum learning experiences for the students.

8. Clarifies skill/s being taught, when required.

9. Encourages students to think and to problem solve.

10. Stimulates student participation through the use of indirect (direct) techniques of providing information.

C. Educational Practices

1. Uses sound motivational techniques during the lesson, incorporating a positive feeling tone (level of concern, high interest level, knowledge of results, expectation of success).

2. Keeps abreast of, and communicates, contemporary issues as they pertain to the students and their world (e.g., environmental concerns, health issues, family relationships, and local, state, and national events).

3. Performs duties in a manner consistent with sound ethical and professional practices.

4. Uses creative methods to encourage greater interest (understanding, comprehension, etc.) by the students.

5. Delivery of information reflects curriculum (course guide) recommended sequence.

6. Incorporates fundamental elements of the basic skills into the lesson (planning, program, etc.).

7. Establishes partnerships (cooperative learning groups, discussion groups, etc.).

8. Makes use of an array of manipulative and/or hands-on aids in the teaching of (name subject area or project activity).

9. Seeks to involve parents in (classroom activities, home projects, school-related activities, the learning process, etc.).

10. Establishes functional (well-maintained, effective) (name subject area) learning center/s.

Vocabulary Aids

This section has been supplied to assist you with the optional rewriting of any of the suggested statements found in the Guide. Searching for that one word that best expresses the thought you wish to convey? Use the Vocabulary Aids section and put that word right at your fingertips!!

adaptability	earnest	precise
adept	energetic	precision
advocate	energy	preparation
aggressive	excite	presence
ambitious	expound on	pretentious
animation	exuberant	proficiency
aplomb	fervent	proficient
articulate	function	progress
assiduous	grow	readiness
assignment	growth	receptivity
assurance	impact	refined
bearing	improve	reform
calm	incisive	reserved
capable	incite	responsible
carriage	influence	robust
clarity	interest	self-confidence
command	leadership	sequential
comment	lesson	sincere
compliance	lethargic	smooth
composure	loquacious	spirited
concern for	mentor	stamina
confidence	mindful	strength
consciousness	model	style
cooperative	modify	supportive
countenance	motivate	technique
course	observant	tendency to
creative	observe	theme
demeanor	orientation	tonality
demonstrate	pace	topic
demonstrative	painstaking	unpretentious
design	passive	vibrant
develop	perfected	vigor
dignity	performance	willing
discernment	perturbed	willingness
drive	plan	

Suggested "Pats on the Back"

This section is geared to provide you with ideas for choosing just the right words to applaud exemplary performance. We hope you will have cause to make liberal use of Suggested "Pats on the Back."

A. (Teacher's name) demonstrates a high degree of professionalism in the performance of his/her teaching duties.

B. (Teacher's name) keeps abreast of current educational reform trends through his/her attendance at seminars (workshops, conferences, courses, etc.).

C. Time is very effectively utilized and managed in your classroom!

D. You are to be commended on your high level of expertise in (describe area of excellence).

E. It is a pleasure to visit a classroom in which the elements of sound teaching, motivated students, and a positive learning environment are so effectively combined.

F. Your presentation was well received and captured the interest of all of the students.

G. You are to be commended for your resolve in remaining on task and maximizing the opportunity for your students to learn (succeed, excel, etc.).

H. Your lesson was creative (innovative) and clearly motivated the students to want to participate (learn).

I. Your students appeared eager, motivated, and happy in your classroom.

J. Your use of (name A-V, manipulative, demonstration, etc.) greatly enhanced the students' understanding of the lesson (skill, objective, etc.).

K. You give evidence of being on the cutting edge of (name trend, educational reform, activity, etc.).

L. Community/School resources are fully used to enhance opportunities for the success of your students.

M. You are an excellent teacher. Strive to maintain your excellent performance level.

N. The best of sound professional practices have been exhibited during this lesson. Keep up the good work!

O. Your participation in school-based activities is highly commendable and greatly appreciated. Thank you!

Section 5

INTERACTION/CLIMATE

This section assists the administrator/supervisor in determining if classroom practices and procedures promote a climate conducive to learning and the promotion of positive self-esteem in students.

Performance statements in this section include

A. Educational Practices
B. Rapport With Students
C. Student Self-Esteem
D. Professional Demeanor
E. Student Management
F. Physical Plant/Equipment and Supplies

Performance Statements

A. Educational Practices

1. Supports student involvement in apprenticeship programs (school-based activities, special projects, training programs, etc.).

2. Provides the opportunity for students to engage in independent reading activities (experiments, projects, etc.) of their own choice.

3. Provides for experiential activities that enable students to gain greater understanding.

4. Works in partnership with parents in the students' best interests.

5. Plans and implements student recognition activities (program, projects).

6. Demonstrates an understanding of current educational issues.

7. Reviews professional journals (texts, periodicals).

8. Demonstrates a comprehensive knowledge of the subject area/s.

9. Provides constructive criticism/s with positive feedback.

10. Demonstrates creativity (imagination, innovation, flexibility, competence, etc.).

B. Rapport With Students

1. Demonstrates concern and respect for students.

2. Maintains an excellent rapport with the students.

3. Respects individual differences in the culture (temperament, learning styles, etc.) of the students without compromising classroom objectives.

4. Demonstrates mutual respect between teacher and students.

5. Assumes primary (secondary) instructional role as resource person (standard-bearer, inspirer, mentor, enforcer of codes, lecturer, counselor, etc.) for students.

6. Demonstrates a knowledge of multicultural issues and their influence on students' adjustment (learning, self-esteem, etc.).

7. Maintains a positive feeling tone.

8. Communicates students' progress to (with) them.

9. Accepts varied viewpoints and adopts a nonjudgmental attitude (manner).

10. Demonstrates an awareness of the uniqueness (value, contribution, etc.) of each student.

C. Student Self-Esteem

1. Exhibits fairness and patience toward students.

2. Encourages collaboration among students through (describe activity, incentive, etc.).

3. Incorporates elements of informal teachings regarding self-esteem (fair practices, tolerance, etc.) into daily classroom activities.

4. Offers praise and encouragement to the students.

5. Provides correction for incorrect responses in a manner conducive to maintaining positive self-esteem in students.

6. Respects the cultural diversity of students.

7. Employs instructional techniques geared toward enhancing positive self-esteem of students.

8. Demonstrates an acceptance of students' thoughts and feelings.

9. Assists students in developing sensitivities for the cultural diversity of others.

10. Recognizes students' needs in terms of their social, emotional, and cultural diversity.

D. Professional Demeanor

1. Maintains contact with parents (teachers, agencies, specialists) regarding student concerns.

2. Exhibits collegiality toward colleagues.

3. Maintains an excellent rapport with students (parents, colleagues, administrators, etc.).

4. Accepts additional responsibilities when required.

5. Shares relevant information with colleagues (parents, students, etc.).

6. Exercises the option of participating in the decision-making process of (name school activity).

7. Voluntarily engages in activities that serve to support and assist students (colleagues, community groups, etc.).

8. Uses knowledge of students to provide educational and social history input during referrals (consultations, etc.).

9. Is knowledgeable of, and uses the aid of, specialists within the school (school system) on behalf of the students.

10. Conducts self in a manner that clearly demonstrates that the welfare of students is of primary importance.

E. Student Management

1. Fosters individual and/or collective responsibility for maintaining a positive environment conducive to learning.

2. Demonstrates the ability to establish effective intervention techniques with students.

3. Uses sound behavior modification techniques.

4. Assumes "case management" role on behalf of students when required.

5. Corrects inappropriate behaviors (responses) without disturbing the learning process.

6. Makes all students active participants in the activities of the classroom.

7. Recognizes the indication for, and implements procedures for, obtaining testing (evaluation, consultation, counseling, etc.) for students experiencing a need for special services.

8. Provides for a smooth transition between subjects (classes, skills).

9. Ensures engagement of all students in the activities of the classroom (group).

10. Creates and uses effective behavior modification (mediation) through (describe strategy).

F. Physical Plant/Equipment and Supplies

1. Fosters individual (collective) responsibilities for maintaining a clean, organized classroom environment.

2. Requires students to respect and maintain their (classroom, group, etc.) supplies and materials.

3. Assigns duties on a rotating basis to foster ownership of classroom responsibilities.

4. Is consistent in ensuring that all students are equipped with sufficient and/or prescribed supplies (textbooks, consumable materials, etc.).

5. Provides bulletin boards that are creatively arranged and well maintained.

6. Gives care and attention to standards of cleanliness, repair, and maintenance regarding custodial services.

7. Promptly reports deficiencies in classroom maintenance (cleanliness, repair, etc.) to proper school division head.

8. Provides for well-maintained learning centers.

9. Motivates students through creative and aesthetic displays.

10. Maintains a classroom environment conducive to maximizing student achievement.

Vocabulary Aids

This section has been supplied to assist you with the optional rewriting of any of the suggested statements found in the Guide. Searching for that one word that best expresses the thought you wish to convey? Use the Vocabulary Aids section and put that word right at your fingertips!!

abusive	diplomatic	mindful
acquiescent	disapprove	motivate
adaptable	discernment	opinionated
advice	discretion	perception
aggressive	discrimination	perceptive
allegiance	divergent	persistent
allied with	dominant	pliant
angry	drive	presence
annoyed	duty	pretentious
arrogant	effective	preside over
astute	emotion	proponent of

attitude   encourage   reactionary
bias   equitable   reasonable
biased   ethical   receptive
bolster   excite   refined
care   feeling tone   regard for
careful   finesse   reproach
changeable   flexible   reserved
character   friendly   respect
collaborate   giving   responsible
comment   govern   reticent
common sense   grace   sagacity
compliant   hardworking   self-confident
composed   honesty   selfish
concern   impression   selfless
confidence   inclination   spirit
congenial   inconsiderate   stable
connection   influence   stamina
cooperative   interchange   strengthen
cordial   interpretation   supervise
criticism   irate   supportive
dedication   judgment   take charge of
demanding   justice   understand
demeanor   justify   unified
denounce   leadership   unpleasant
deportment   lenient   unpretentious
devious   logic   upset
devotion   logical   veracity
dignified   loyal   vigor
dignity   manipulate

Suggested "Pats on the Back"

This section is geared to provide you with ideas for choosing just the right words to applaud exemplary performance. We hope you will have cause to make liberal use of Suggested "Pats on the Back."

A. It is evident that mutual respect exists between you and your students.
B. Your students benefit greatly from the exceptional way in which you volunteer extra time and effort to support (tutor, advise, etc.) them.
C. You have succeeded in molding a spirit of cohesion among students of diverse backgrounds and cultures.
D. Your "firm but fair" demeanor is highly effective in maintaining a sense of direction and purpose in your students.
E. (Teacher's name) freely gives praise when it is deserved.

F. There is a feeling of well-being and conviviality in your classroom.

G. You promote honest discussion among your students, which flourishes in the overall climate of trust and support.

H. You excellently demonstrate a flair for rendering constructive criticism in a positive and considerate manner.

I. You are to be commended for your involvement in the school extra-curricular program (name other special project/s).

J. The learning center/s (bulletin boards, posters, charts, etc.) serve to enhance the climate and opportunity for the students to learn and thrive.

K. It is very apparent that (teacher's name) is highly focused and has the best interests of his/her students as a primary consideration.

L. (Teacher's name) serves as a role model for his/her students (counselees, colleagues, community, etc.).

M. (Teacher's name) is highly skilled in maintaining sound disciplinary (and/or academic) standards.

N. Your classroom is a model for exhibiting the benefits that can be gained when there is diversity of cultures (ideas, backgrounds, etc.).

O. (Teacher's name) is a great asset to (name of school). Keep up the good work!

Part 2

OTHER HELPFUL RESOURCES FOR WRITING PERFORMANCE EVALUATIONS

This section contains

- Common Areas of Concern, With Suggested Remedies
- The Evaluation Organizer
- Sample Written Evaluations, With Commentary
- Cross-Reference of Key Terms
- Chronology of Evaluation Activities
- Record of Evaluations
- A Checklist of Basic Documentation and/or Conditions

Section 6

COMMON AREAS OF CONCERN, WITH SUGGESTED REMEDIES

Problem 1.

Teacher failed to communicate expectations of the lesson to the students.

Suggestions:

a. Instructional objective/s of each lesson must be clearly posted (articulated).

b. Provide (Elicit) an information base to be utilized when introducing new concepts.

c. Employ anticipatory set activities to enhance students' focus and understanding.

d. Model sample activities to illustrate expected outcomes.

e. Give timely and helpful feedback to students.

Problem 2.

Evidence needed that students learned what was expected.

Suggestions:

a. Test for comprehension (mastery) using a variety of techniques.

b. Assess understanding before progressing to the next level.

c. Maintain student records (assessment documentation, files, portfolios, folders, etc.) up to the highest professional standards.

d. Give timely feedback to students on their homework assignments.

e. Check homework as a means of assessing mastery.

Problem 3.

Little teacher-directed instruction was observed.

Suggestions:

a. Place limits on the amount of chalkboard seatwork given as a tool for practice (assessing understanding).
b. Reteach skill/s when needed.

Problem 4.

Teacher's skills are deficient.

Suggestions:

a. Address skill deficiencies outlined in your previous (conference, observation, discussion).
b. Vary method/s of instruction to promote students' interest (participation) in the lesson.
c. Use a variety of approaches to delivery of instruction.
d. Become knowledgeable about standard educational (school) policies and procedures.
e. Consistently implement standard (school) policies and procedures.
f. Take advantage of professional development opportunities to enhance professional abilities.
g. Take prompt action to remedy outlined area/s of weakness (deficiency).
h. Diversify instructional techniques to effectively address the varied learning styles of the students.

Problem 5.

Students displayed little motivation to learn.

Suggestions:

a. Plan and implement activities relevant to students' developmental levels.
b. Make every attempt to relate learning to the students' life experiences.
c. Encourage students to explore and search for understanding (relevancy).

d. Implement and maintain a classroom environment that is conducive to learning.

e. Establish a peer assistance program to enhance the students' opportunities for achievement.

f. Devise methods to motivate reticent students to participate.

g. Prepare individual assignments that challenge students.

h. Provide students with opportunities to succeed.

i. Provide opportunities for all students to participate through awareness and planning for their varied learning styles.

j. Avoid long pauses during presentation.

k. Accelerate the pace of presentation of facts.

l. Eliminate classroom interruptions and maximize time-on-task.

m. Use a variety of materials (techniques) geared toward motivating students.

n. Encourage all students to participate actively in classroom (discussions, activities, planning, etc.).

o. Secure and maintain students' attention and participation.

p. Ensure preparedness of all students relative to class supplies and appropriate texts.

q. Employ use of appropriate supplemental aids (A-V) to stimulate interest (understanding, etc.).

Problem 6.

Lesson ended abruptly with little follow-up.

Suggestions:

a. Relate homework (seatwork) assignments to classroom activities.

b. Allow sufficient time for students to process acquired information.

c. Phrase question/s to test for student understanding (comprehension, comfort zone, etc.).

d. Assign follow-up activities (homework, seatwork, research projects, etc.).

e. Allow sufficient time for students to practice acquired skills.

f. Allow sufficient time for closure activities.

Problem 7.

Students failed to accomplish the stated lesson objectives.

Suggestions:

a. Promote cognitive learning through a variety of techniques, such as (suggest technique/s and/or give an example).
b. Promote inferential learning through a variety of techniques, such as (suggest technique/s and/or give an example).
c. Lead students to an awareness of the incremental progress being made toward meeting the objectives of the lesson.
d. Provide students with creative and high-interest activities to stimulate learning.

Problem 8.

Supplemental resource aids were not utilized.

Suggestions:

a. Generate teacher-made materials (aids) to supplement textbook (workbook) material.
b. Use supplemental materials to enhance understanding.
c. Provide opportunities for hands-on experiences for students.
d. Use (Increase use of) the services of the teacher's aide to facilitate reaching goals.
e. Use the assistance of appropriate school-based specialists (resource persons, etc.).
f. Use appropriate A-V materials to enhance the lesson.

Problem 9.

Students were given too little direction.

Suggestions:

a. Delineate focus and provide direction when giving independent assignments.
b. Monitor students' seatwork on an ongoing basis.
c. Monitor students' progress throughout the lesson.
d. Provide individual (group) assistance when needed.
e. Check students' (notebooks, notes, etc.) to ensure that study material will be at an acceptable level of accuracy and neatness.

Problem 10.

Students were given too much direction.

Suggestions:

a. Suggest that there be less reliance on the teacher-as-lecturer method as the sole technique of instruction.
b. Allow students the freedom to explore varied methods of reaching the lesson's objectives.

Problem 11.

Teacher remains isolated. No school spirit demonstrated.

Suggestions:

a. Share successful techniques with colleagues.
b. Keep current with knowledge of educational reform (movement, techniques, strategies, etc.).
c. Attend (workshops, seminars, etc.) and share information with colleagues.

Problem 12.

Planning was insufficient and/or unavailable.

Suggestions:

a. Include planning geared toward varied learning styles of students.
b. Keep plans congruent to the stated objective/s.
c. Formulate clear and comprehensive instructional objectives.
d. Maintain timely and comprehensive plans.
e. Have plans available at all times.
f. Maintain timely and comprehensive record/s of students' (achievements, weaknesses, strengths, progress, etc.).
g. Maintain plans reflective of the highest professional standards of expertise.
h. Design learning objectives and activities reflective of the high expectations held for students.

Problem 13.

Class was disorderly. Poor discipline.

Suggestions:

a.   Develop and implement a sound classroom code of conduct.

b.   Consistently enforce the classroom code of conduct.

c.   Develop strategies to resolve student conflict/s.

d.   Develop behavior modification (plans, strategies, activities, etc.) geared toward changing negative behaviors.

e.   Eliminate choral response activities and require individual students to respond to posed questions.

f.   Seek support and assistance from (colleagues, administration, counselors, parents, etc.) in working toward a healthy and productive classroom environment.

g.   Request a conference with (parents, student/s, administration, outside agency, school resource persons, etc.) regarding the negative behavior/s of the student/s.

Problem 14.

Teacher had a poor relationship with students.

Suggestions:

a.   Display tact and understanding when resolving conflict situations.

b.   Develop strategies to resolve student conflict.

c.   Respect and value the opinions (beliefs, viewpoint/s, misgivings, etc.) of the students.

d.   Respect and value the multicultural composition of the students in the class.

e.   Recognize and validate the contributions of students who volunteer information.

f.   Formulate strategies to enhance a positive relationship with the students.

g.   Develop activities (strategies) that allow students to gain some (autonomy, recognition, etc.).

Section 7 🖉

THE EVALUATION ORGANIZER

The Evaluation Organizer is offered as a tool to expedite the use of the Guide. Specifically, the organizer sheets and your copy of *Writing Meaningful Teacher Evaluations—Right Now!!* are all you need as you monitor the delivery of instruction in your school.

The format of the organizer allows you to use a form of shorthand to record statements that will be used on your approved evaluation instrument. In the example below, we see how the organizer is used to record statements from just one of the performance areas:

Section 4: Instructional Performance

"Pat on the Back"

A7	B8	C8							I	

We can now decode these Instructional Performance statements as:

A7 - Provides ample "wait time" in order to encourage all learners to participate.

B8 - Clarifies skill/s being taught when required.

C8 - Utilizes an array of manipulative and/or hands-on aids in the teaching of (description of the observed activity).

The instructor is also praised by using a statement from the Suggested "Pats on the Back" area in the Instructional Performance section, that is,

I - Your students appeared eager, motivated, and happy in your classroom.

EVALUATION ORGANIZER

Name: _____   Date: _____

                                          [ ] Tenured   [ ] Informal Observation

Grade/Subject: _____   [ ] Nontenured [ ] Evaluation

Evaluator: _____   Time: _____

Section 1: Proficiency With Curriculum   "Pat on the Back"

Section 2: Evaluating Student Growth   "Pat on the Back"

Section 3: Preparation and Readiness   "Pat on the Back"

Section 4: Instructional Performance   "Pat on the Back"

Section 5: Interaction/Climate   "Pat on the Back"

Special Notes: _____

_____

Suggestion: Duplicate multiple copies in advance of observations/evaluations.

Section 8

SAMPLE WRITTEN EVALUATIONS, WITH COMMENTARY

The quality of an informal and/or formal evaluation may be influenced by a wide range of variables. It is the task of the observer to consistently provide the staff being evaluated with fair, substantive, and highly credible evaluations.

Note how the fictitious evaluations included in this section demonstrate a rich combination of phrases found in the Guide with specific references to activities observed during a lesson.

The formal evaluation format varies widely between districts. This Guide is adaptable and highly appropriate for any of them! With the Guide and an Evaluation Organizer sheet, you will be able to produce quality staff performance documents . . . on time . . . every time!

SCHOOL SYSTEM OF ANYTOWN, U.S.A.
Staff Evaluation Report

NAME: Ms. New & Magnificent   **SCHOOL:** Very Lucky School

ASSIGNMENT: Teacher, Grade 4   **DATE:** 0/00/00

SUBJECT: Social Studies

OBJECTIVE: To understand the system of governance and the function of major departments of city government.

Rate subject on scale of:

A	B	C	D
Demonstrates Excellence	Good	Fair	Unsatisfactory

I.	Preparation	A	IV.	Indicators of Academic Growth	A
II.	Delivery	A	V.	Learning Environment	A
III.	Demeanor	A	VI.	Affective Domain	A

SUMMARY OF OBSERVED LESSON: Opening exercises were purposeful and geared toward establishing a concrete framework for presentation of new skills. Ms. M clearly explained the lesson objectives and learning tasks. Each group chairperson was to report on the findings of group research into city governance. She involved students in the art of reinforcing knowledge and skills through allowing them to demonstrate their researching skill with the reading of reports about the training and duties of their chosen "city worker." She gave students the opportunity to ask questions of their class-mates. Ms. M promoted positive self-esteem through praise and encourage-ment.

AREAS OF COMMENDATION: Ms. M is to be commended for assisting stu-dents in the development of critical thinking skills to access information re-garding their topics. Activities were kept congruent to the objectives of the lesson. Each group leader led the group through the five steps of a prepared outline for making concise and comprehensive reports. She conducted evalu-ations of the content knowledge of students by engaging them in discussion and question-answer sessions.

SUGGESTED IMPROVEMENTS: The success of this unit of study might be strengthened through the inclusion of guest lecturers who are within the city government systems that have been researched. Establish seating arrange-ments appropriate for the activities of the lesson, requiring individual stu-dents to read reports while others critique.

EVALUATION SUMMARY: Ms. M maintains a learning environment that contributes to the positive feeling of self-worth of the students. The opening activities were purposeful and geared toward establishing a concrete framework for presentation of new skills. Ms. M assisted and challenged students to become self-directed learners by providing opportunities for self-evaluation. She kept students focused and actively participating in the lesson through varied activities, including writing letters to agencies, erecting a cardboard floorplan of City Hall, and organizing a field trip to the Parks Department. Time-on-task was maximized. Students' written reports and drawings were displayed.

NO NAME SCHOOL DISTRICT, EVERYWHERE, U.S.A.

NAME: Mr. Long On Staff   **SCHOOL:**   Medium Middle School

POSITION: Teacher-Physical Education   **DATE:**   0/00/00

OBJECTIVE: To teach the fundamentals of the game of soccer

Grade 7   Enrollment: 17   Present: 11

1 = Exceptional   2 = Average   3 = Improvement Needed   4 = Unsatisfactory

A. Preparation   3   E. Environment   2

B. Presentation   3   F. Organization   3

C. Student Management   3   G. Affective Domain   3

D. Growth Indicators   3

COMMENDATIONS: Mr. S is dependable and consistent in reporting to school duty assignments on time.

He serves as coach of the school's intramural volleyball teams.

He also voluntarily engages in activities that serve to support and assist community groups in their after-school centers.

The gymnasium is healthfully aerated at all times.

LESSON FOCAL POINTS: In opening the lesson, Mr. S failed to communicate directions or model the required activities. Students were observed entering the gym and streaming onto the play area without any form of attendance, inspection, or organization being imposed.

While the lesson objective was posted on the portable chalkboard, during the observed lesson, activities failed to reflect the objective of the lesson.

The opening activities were not purposeful or geared toward establishing a concrete framework for presentation of new skills needed for soccer.

Mr. S did attempt to implement strategies to motivate the students to learn through the demonstration of a few running and kicking moves. He failed to vary the instructional techniques in order to accommodate the varied learning styles of the group.

A few students were observed disrupting others as they attempted to remain on task.

Mr. S failed to command the attention and cooperation of all students in the class. Mr. S maintained a nonaggressive manner with the students. Neither the planbook nor the rollbook was readily available for reference or for the recording of student progress.

Mr. S did not demonstrate competence or ease during the evaluation session.

COMMENTS AND/OR SUGGESTIONS: It is necessary to clearly explain the lesson and learning tasks to the students. Begin class with material related to the prior lesson/s, providing students with transfer information to establish the basis for them to understand the new skills.

Consistently communicate directions and model the required activities when needed. There was need to provide a sequential array of learning activities, ensuring that the desired goals of learning the fundamentals of soccer were reached.

Maintain focus by teaching to the objectives. Monitor students' work and provide timely feedback indicating what they can do to improve their performance. Vary your instructional style in accordance with student needs.

Maintain a planbook that is comprehensive and up-to-date. Maintain a current, legible, and comprehensive rollbook. Both planbook and rollbook must be readily available for reference and for recording students' progress.

Incorporate fundamental elements of the basic skills into your planning.

Ensure the engagement of all students in the activities of the group. Demonstrate the ability to establish effective intervention techniques with students. Recognize and control negative behaviors through the preparation of mandatory written assignments for unprepared students. In addition, engage their participation in classroom activities through the setting-up and care of equipment, scorekeeping, and recording the rules and regulations of the activity. Support and reinforce on-task behaviors.

Facilitate students' channeling of disruptive feelings through the comprehensive planning and implementation of creative and productive activities in which all students will feel motivated to participate.

Maintain high expectations and communicate them clearly to all students.

Maintain a learning environment that contributes to the positive feeling of self-worth in the students. Incorporate into daily classroom activities elements of informal teaching regarding fair practices and consideration for others. Maintain contact with parents regarding student concerns.

Post-Evaluation Conference Scheduled for: _____

Please Bring: 1. _____

2. _____

3. _____

4. _____

5. _____

_____	_____	_____	_____
Teacher	Date	Evaluator/Title	Date

TEACHER PROFILE: This staff member is a veteran of more than 25 years and is well known and respected in the community. He is personable and congenial. The quality of his instructional performance has declined over the years.

PLEASE NOTE: In this evaluation, statements were taken directly from the Guide and used to formulate suggestions for improving a marginal performance.

METROPOLITAN SCHOOL DISTRICT, EVERYWHERE, U.S.A.

NAME: Ms. New Teacher   **SCHOOL:** P.S. #01

POSITION: Teacher, Grade 7   DATE 0/00/00

SUBJECT: Mathematics

LESSON OBJECTIVE: Basic Algebra: Finding the value of X

1 = Exceptional   2 = Average   3 = Improvement Needed   4 = Unsatisfactory

A.	Preparation	2	E.	Environment	2
B.	Presentation	3	F.	Organization	3
C.	Student Management	3	G.	Affective Domain	2
D.	Growth Indicators	3			

COMMENDATIONS: Ms. T demonstrates a mature response to constructive suggestions and seeks to effect positive change in the area of her mathematics assignment.

She demonstrates an acceptance of students' thoughts and feelings.

Ms. T is to be commended for her service as coordinator of P.S. #1's regional mathematics elementary quiz bowl for the current school year.

OBSERVATION ANALYSIS: Ms. T began the lesson with a synopsis of the instructional objective and its correlation to the lesson's objective.

The activity of copying the textbook description of the method of finding the value of an unknown number was completed next.

Ms. T failed to convey her excitement regarding the subject matter to the students using this method.

Examples of algebraic problems were demonstrated on the chalkboard prior to the students being asked to demonstrate proficiency. Ms. T failed to challenge students to understand the process by which answers are reached. Ms. T failed to invite questions or to encourage the students to challenge the examples.

Throughout the observed lesson, Ms. T continued to teach facts in isolation. She did not employ strategies to gain attention and maintain students' focus on the lesson.

It must be noted that Ms. T avoids negative criticisms.

Teacher made posters and charts that complemented and supported the curriculum activities were displayed.

Ms. T has established a well-maintained mathematics learning center.

The planbook was readily available for reference. Alternative plans for students of varied competencies were not provided.

Ms. T respects the cultural diversity of her students. She also assists students to develop sensitivity for the cultural diversity of others.

COMMENTS/SUGGESTIONS: It is good that you began the lesson with a synopsis of the instructional objective and its correlation to the lesson's objective.

To complement this, you must clearly *explain* the lesson objectives and learning tasks. Furthermore, you must communicate expectations for learning.

Some suggested strategies for improvement would be:

1. To begin the class with material related to prior lessons, providing students with transfer information that will provide them with a basis for learning the new skills.

2. To provide a sequential array of learning activities, ensuring that the goals are reached.

3. To challenge students to *understand the process* by which answers are reached.

4. To use a variety of activities and materials to address varied learning styles.

5. To allow students to collaborate to gain understanding.

6. To encourage students to ask questions and seek assistance when needed.

7. To give students ample opportunities to demonstrate comprehension of the subject matter.

8. To circulate among the students, offering assistance.

9. To accurately measure the degree to which student learning meets the objective of the lesson.

10. To provide alternative plans for students of varied competencies.

11. To vary instructional style in accordance with student needs.

You are to be commended on your knowledge of multicultural issues and their effect on students' self-esteem. Make all students active participants in the activities of the classroom. Encourage students to take pride in their accomplishments.

Use the aid of specialists within the school on behalf of the students who are experiencing difficulties.

Participate in professional group activities in order to add to your knowledge base of "good ideas."

    She has an advanced degree in mathematics.

    She is eager and receptive to all efforts made to assist her in improving her performance.

SIGNATURE OF STAFF MEMBER: _____ DATE: _____

SIGNATURE OF SUPERVISOR: _____ DATE: _____

TEACHER PROFILE: This staff member is in the third year of her appointment to an elementary school departmental position.

PLEASE NOTE: In this evaluation, additional demonstration is given of the technique of using statements from the Guide as the framework for giving concrete suggestions for improvement of performance.

METROPOLITAN SCHOOL DISTRICT, EVERYWHERE, U.S.A.

NAME: Ms. Very Experienced   **SCHOOL:** Apple Pie High

POSITION: Teacher   **DATE:** 0/00/00

SUBJECT: Freshman English

LESSON OBJECTIVE: Understanding the main idea using textbook passages and supplemental text (Boise's Tale)

1 = Exceptional   2 = Average   3 = Improvement Needed   4 = Unsatisfactory

A. Preparation	2	E. Environment	2
B. Presentation	2	F. Organization	2
C. Student Management	2	G. Affective Domain	2
D. Growth Indicators	2		

COMMENDATIONS: Ms. E serves as chairperson of the district's Parent-Teacher Alliance Association. She also voluntarily engages in activities that serve to support and assist students who have suffered traumatic home experiences that have led to difficulties at school.

She participates in professional group activities sponsored by the English Department.

Ms. E recognizes students' needs in terms of their social, emotional, and cultural diversities.

COMMENTS: Ms. E followed the approved district curriculum. The curriculum guide was used to plan detailed lesson plans. The activities were kept congruent to the objectives of the lesson. This was demonstrated by the oral discussion and the plotting of the story line of "Boise's Tale" by the students in their workbooks. After this exercise, Ms. E posed questions at the literal level of comprehension. She teaches for cognitive learning.

Ms. E performs her duties in a manner consistent with sound ethical and professional practices. She demonstrates highly professional speaking skills.

Ms. E maintains records that are accurate, thorough, and up-to-date. A review of the planbook indicated that she had planned for enrichment activities. Most of the class period was taken up by the discussion and the seatwork. (From "Special Notes" section of the log sheet.) As a result, Ms. E was unable to check for understanding before distributing written assignments for homework.

OBSERVATIONS/SUGGESTIONS: The basic premise of the lesson was well founded.

To enhance your established expertise in teaching English, it is suggested that you employ anticipatory set activities to enhance students' focus and understanding. Assess understanding before progressing to the next level. Place limits on the amount of seatwork given as tools for practice. Diversify your instructional technique to effectively address the varied learning styles of the students. Employ the use of appropriate A-V to stimulate interest. Allow sufficient time for closure activities.

Promote inferential learning through a variety of techniques. Check students' notes to ensure that study materials will be at an acceptable level of accuracy and neatness.

Suggest there be less reliance on the teacher-as-lecturer method as the sole technique of instruction. Share successful techniques with colleagues.

TEACHER PROFILE: The staff member for whom this evaluation was made is one year away from her retirement. She has enjoyed a career spanning 25 years. Many changes have ensued during her long tenure in the Metropolitan School District.

Her instructional delivery, which was always adequate, has remained essentially the same throughout her long career. She has been known to disavow many of the "young people's" approaches to instructional delivery.

PLEASE NOTE: In this evaluation, all of the suggestions are taken from the "Common Areas of Concern With Suggested Remedies" section.

SCHOOL SYSTEM OF ANYTOWN, U.S.A.
Staff Evaluation Report

NAME: Mr. Great Potential   **SCHOOL:** Outdoorsey High

ASSIGNMENT: Teacher   **DATE:**   0/00/00

SUBJECT: Science

OBJECTIVE: Biology—To understand the process of osmosis through experimentation

Rate evaluatee on scale of:

A	B	C	D
Demonstrates Excellence	Good	Fair	Unsatisfactory

I. Preparation	A	IV.	Indicators of Academic Growth	A
II. Delivery	A	V.	Learning Environment	A
III. Demeanor	A	VI.	Affective Domain	A

SUMMARY OF OBSERVED LESSON: Mr. P began the lesson with the dissemination of review material containing previously acquired skills in which cells were studied. This related the lesson content to prior learning.

Activities were varied to increase the understanding of lesson concepts. After the review, Mr. P invited questions and encouraged students to challenge the concepts. He then used A-V (a short filmstrip demonstrating osmosis activity) to enhance understanding. The materials were well chosen and effective for working with students with varied learning styles.

The enthusiastic presentation kept students focused and actively participating in the lesson.

During the hands-on experiment phase of the lesson, Mr. P clearly defined the lesson requirements to the students. He inspired students through the creative experiential method of presentation of the subject matter.

He provided timely and constructive feedback and conducted ongoing checks for comprehension.

He conveyed excitement regarding the subject matter—which was transferred to the students.

Mr. P involved his students in the art of discovery through the experiment in which they watched molecules travel through cell membranes. The students were allowed to collaborate to gain understanding regarding their progress.

Mr. P checked for understanding before distributing written assignments.

Mr. P provided a sequential array of learning activities, ensuring that the desired goals were reached.

He demonstrated a comprehensive knowledge of the subject area. He motivated students to learn through the extensive interest he brought to the subject.

AREAS OF COMMENDATION: You made the lesson "come alive" for the students. You adeptly led the students through the discovery process and on to a logical conclusion. Students were given excellent and timely feedback regarding their experiments.

You demonstrated creativity and skill in your method of assessing comprehension of the lesson. It is evident that a great deal of planning and preparation went into your lesson. Good work!

Your lesson was innovative and clearly motivated the students to want to learn. You are to be commended on your high level of expertise in the teaching of science.

It is a pleasure to visit a classroom in which the elements of sound teaching, motivated students, and a positive learning environment are so effectively combined.

Mr. P is a great asset to Outdoorsey High School. Keep up the good work!

SUGGESTED IMPROVEMENTS: Consider serving as the coordinator of the upcoming school science fair.

By now you must be raring to go!! In reading the evaluations that have been compiled for you, we're sure you noticed many other statements that could have been chosen to convey the same thoughts. That's one of the many benefits of the Guide! You'll never be at a loss for words!

By the way—all of the statements in "areas of commendation" were taken from the suggested "Pats on the Back" section of the Guide.

Section 9

CROSS-REFERENCE OF KEY TERMS

WORD/PHRASE	LOCATION IN GUIDE
Acceptance	Sec.5-C8
Accomplishment	Sec.2-C1
Accountability	Sec.2-D2
Accurate	Sec.1-B9
Achievement	Sec.2-D4
Activities	Sec.1-A5, A10, B6, B8, B10, D2, D9, E4, E6, G2, G7; Sec.5-A3, A5, A9
Alternatives	Sec.3-A9
Appearance	Sec.3-C4
Application	Sec.1-B4,G4
Apprenticeship	Sec.5-A1
Assessment	Sec.1-E1, E3, F1; Sec.2-A7, B10, F2, F3
Assistance	Sec.1-F4, F5
Attendance	Sec.3-C5, C6
Authority	Sec.2-C5
A.V. Materials	Sec.1-B7; Sec.3-B5
Basic Skills	Sec.4-C6
Behavior	Sec.5-E5
Behavior Modification	Sec.5-E3, E10
Bulletin Boards	Sec.5-F5
Case Management	Sec.5-E4
Cement	Sec.1-G1
Chalkboard	Sec.2-A3
Challenges	Sec.1-C4, G5
Child-Centered	Sec.3-C9; Sec.4-A5
Child's Feeling	Sec.1-A1
Circulate	Sec.2-B9
Clarify	Sec.4-B8
Class Environment	Sec.5-F10
Class Maintenance	Sec.5-F7
Cleanliness	Sec.5-F6
Climate	Sec.1-G3; Sec.3-C2

WORD/PHRASE	*LOCATION IN GUIDE*
Closure	Sec.1-G7
Cognitive Development	Sec.1-E4
Collaboration	Sec.5-C2
Colleagues	Sec.5-D2, D5
Collegiality	Sec.5-D2
Commands	Sec.4-A8
Communicate	Sec.1-A5, A9, D8, F5
Competency	Sec.2-D1; Sec.3-A9
Comprehension	Sec.1-E1, E2; Sec.2-B1, B4, E4, F1
Concepts	Sec.1-A3, B5, D3
Conclusions	Sec.2-C10
Congruent	Sec.1-B6
Constructive Criticism	Sec.3-C3; Sec.5-A9
Cooperation	Sec.4-A8
Correlation	Sec.1-A8
Creativity	Sec.1-C3, G1; Sec.2-C9, E6; Sec.4-C4; Sec.5-A10, F5, F9
Critical Thinking	Sec.1-E1, E3; Sec.4-B4
Cultural Diversity	Sec.5-C6, C9, C10
Current Issues	Sec.5-A6
Decision Making	Sec.5-D6
Desired Goals	Sec.1-B8, C10
Dignity	Sec.1-G3
Dimensions	Sec.1-B2
Discovery	Sec.1-C9
Dissemination	Sec.1-G8
Encourage	Sec.1-G3; Sec.2-A9, F10; Sec.5-C4
Enhances	Sec.1-B1, C8, E5
Enthusiasm	Sec.1-G2; Sec.2-C7
Environment	Sec.2-B10
Equity	Sec.4-A10
Expectation	Sec.2-C2, C3, D8
Experiences	Sec.1-A1, A7, C3, C5
Fairness	Sec.5-C1
Feedback	Sec.2-A1, A2, A5; Sec.5-A9
Feeling Tone	Sec.5-B7, C8
Focus	Sec.1-D5, E8; Sec.2-A5, D4; Sec.4-A4, B1
Future Learning	Sec.1-A4, D9
Goal Setting	Sec.2-C6; Sec.4-A9
Goals	Sec.2-A7, E3

WORD/PHRASE	*LOCATION IN GUIDE*
Hands-On	Sec.1-E10; Sec.3-B4; Sec.4-C8
Home Study	Sec.1-G8
Homework	Sec.1-G7
Independent	Sec.2-D9; Sec.5-A2
Individual Assistance	Sec.2-B5
Information	Sec.1-F10
Innovative	Sec.2-E5; Sec.3-A3
Instruction	Sec.1-D6
Instructional Techniques	Sec.2-A6; Sec.4-B7; Sec.5-C7
Integrate	Sec.1-D7, E7, E9
Intellectual	Sec.1-E5
Interact	Sec.2-D5
Interdisciplinary	Sec.3-A5
Internalized	Sec.1-G6
Intervention	Sec.5-E2
Knowledge	Sec.1-C8, D1, D3, G1, G4
Learners	Sec.1-G5
Learning	Sec.2-C7, F9
Learning Centers	Sec.1-F6; Sec.4-C10; Sec.5-F8
Learning Process	Sec.1-C1
Learning Situation	Sec.1-C5
Learning Styles	Sec.1-E6; Sec.2-A6; Sec.3-B6; Sec.4-A1
Lecture	Sec.4-A2
Long-Term Goals	Sec.2-D6
Mastery	Sec.2-D7, E7, F6
Materials	Sec.1-D5, D9, G6, G8
Methods	Sec.1-D7; Sec.2-C10
Models	Sec.1-A5
Monitors	Sec.2-B2, B3, B6, F8; Sec.4-B5
Motivation	Sec.1-C1, C2; Sec.2-C8, E3; Sec.4-C1
Multicultural	Sec.5-B6
Nonjudgemental	Sec.5-B9
Objective	Sec.1-A2, A8, B6, B10, E8, F2, F7; Sec.2-E8, F5; Sec.3-A10, B7
Observation	Sec.2-E9, C8
Opportunity	Sec.1-B4, C3, G1, G4
Pacing	Sec.1-F9
Parents	Sec.3-A8; Sec.4-C9; Sec.5-A4, D1

WORD/PHRASE	*LOCATION IN GUIDE*
Participation	Sec.1-G1, G2; Sec.4-A7, A10, B10; Sec.5-E6, E9
Partnerships	Sec.4-C7; Sec.5-A4
Patience	Sec.2-B7; Sec.5-C1
Performances	Sec.1-D4; Sec.2-E6
Planbook	Sec.3-A1, A2, A6, A7
Planning	Sec.3-C7, C9, C10
Practical Life	Sec.1-D3
Praise	Sec.5-C4
Presents Information	Sec.1-B3
Prior Lessons	Sec.1-A6
Problem Solving	Sec.1-E5; Sec.2-A8, D10; Sec.4-B9
Processes Of Discovery	Sec.1-C3, C4
Professional	Sec.1-D4, D10; Sec.3-C2; Sec.4-C3
Proficiency	Sec.2-A3
Progress	Sec.2-D3, D4, E10; Sec.3-B2
Question	Sec.1-E2; Sec.2-A9, E9
Rapport	Sec.5-B2, D3
Realistic Approach	Sec.1-A7
Recognition	Sec.2-E2
Record	Sec.2-E10
Referrals	Sec.5-D8
Reinforcement	Sec.2-B8; Sec.3-B10
Relevancy	Sec.1-C5, C6, F7, G10
Resources	Sec.5-B5
Respect	Sec.5-B1, B3, B4, C6, F2, F3
Responses	Sec.2-B7
Responsibility	Sec.2-C5; Sec.5-D4, E1; Sec.5-F1
Reteach	Sec.1-F8
Review	Sec.1-G8; Sec.5-A7
Role	Sec.5-B5
Rollbook	Sec.2-F7
School Facilities	Sec.1-G10
Seatwork	Sec.1-G10
Self-Esteem	Sec.5-C3, C5, C7
Self-Evaluation	Sec.2-C6, F10; Sec.5-D10
Sequence	Sec.4-C5
Sequential Array	Sec.1-B8, B9
Short-Term Goals	Sec.2-D6
Skills	Sec.1-A3, A6, D5
Smooth Transition	Sec.5-E8
Specialist	Sec.5-D9
Strategies	Sec.1-C1, C2, E5; Sec.3-C1; Sec.4-A4, B3

WORD/PHRASE	*LOCATION IN GUIDE*
Subject Matter	Sec.1-C7, C8, D1, D6, E1, G2; Sec.2-C7
Success	Sec.4-A3
Sufficient Time	Sec.1-G6, G7
Supplementary Materials	Sec.1-B1, C8
Supplies	Sec.5-F4
Synopsis	Sec.1-A8
Tasks	Sec.4-A6
Teacher Aids	Sec.3-B9
Teacher-Directed	Sec.4-A5
Teacher-Made	Sec.3-B8
Technology	Sec.2-E1
Testing	Sec.2-E8; Sec.5-E7
Test-Taking	Sec.2-A10, F4
Think	Sec.1-D7; Sec.2-D10
Thought-Provoking	Sec.1-F3
Understand	Sec.1-C4, C6, G9; Sec.2-E9
Uniqueness	Sec.5-B10
Variety	Sec.2-A4
Visuals	Sec.1-F7; Sec.3-B1
Viewing Skills	Sec.1-D7
Volunteer	Sec.5-D7
"Wait-Time"	Sec.4-A7
Whole Language	Sec.1-D7
Workshops	Sec.1-D1
Written Skills	Sec.1-D8, D10, G9

CHRONOLOGY OF EVALUATION ACTIVITIES*

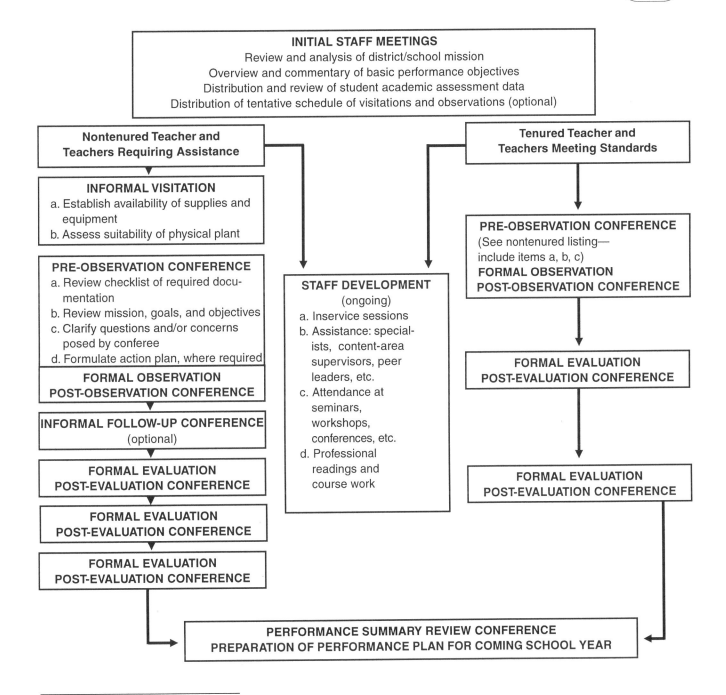

INITIAL STAFF MEETINGS
Review and analysis of district/school mission
Overview and commentary of basic performance objectives
Distribution and review of student academic assessment data
Distribution of tentative schedule of visitations and observations (optional)

Nontenured Teacher and Teachers Requiring Assistance

Tenured Teacher and Teachers Meeting Standards

INFORMAL VISITATION
a. Establish availability of supplies and equipment
b. Assess suitability of physical plant

PRE-OBSERVATION CONFERENCE
a. Review checklist of required documentation
b. Review mission, goals, and objectives
c. Clarify questions and/or concerns posed by conferee
d. Formulate action plan, where required

FORMAL OBSERVATION
POST-OBSERVATION CONFERENCE

INFORMAL FOLLOW-UP CONFERENCE
(optional)

FORMAL EVALUATION
POST-EVALUATION CONFERENCE

FORMAL EVALUATION
POST-EVALUATION CONFERENCE

FORMAL EVALUATION
POST-EVALUATION CONFERENCE

STAFF DEVELOPMENT
(ongoing)
a. Inservice sessions
b. Assistance: specialists, content-area supervisors, peer leaders, etc.
c. Attendance at seminars, workshops, conferences, etc.
d. Professional readings and course work

PRE-OBSERVATION CONFERENCE
(See nontenured listing—include items a, b, c)
FORMAL OBSERVATION
POST-OBSERVATION CONFERENCE

FORMAL EVALUATION
POST-EVALUATION CONFERENCE

FORMAL EVALUATION
POST-EVALUATION CONFERENCE

PERFORMANCE SUMMARY REVIEW CONFERENCE
PREPARATION OF PERFORMANCE PLAN FOR COMING SCHOOL YEAR

* The structure, frequency, and content of evaluation activities are entirely dependent upon requirements formulated by individual districts and the leadership techniques of the evaluator.

Section 11

RECORD OF EVALUATIONS

Name_____ Title_____ School Year_____

NAME	GRADE	TEN.	NONTEN.	OBSER.	PRE.	EVAL.	POST.
1.							
2.							
3.							
4.							
5.							
6.							
7.							
8.							
9.							
10.							
11.							
12.							
13.							
14.							
15.							
16.							
17.							
18.							
19.							
20.							
21.							
22.							
23.							
24.							

Section 12

A CHECKLIST OF BASIC DOCUMENTATION AND/OR CONDITIONS*

TEACHER:_____   SUBJECT/GRADE:_____

DATE:_____/_____/_____

SECTION 1: PROFICIENCY WITH CURRICULUM

_____Core Standards
_____Grade Level Proficiencies
_____Teacher's Edition/s
_____Curriculum Guide/s
_____Supplementary Material/s

SECTION 2: EVALUATING STUDENT GROWTH

_____Scored Test Papers
_____Standardized Test Results
_____Recorded Test Scores
_____Teacher-Made Quizzes
_____Posted Examples of Students' Work
_____Homework Assignments: Graded/Recorded
_____Student Journals
_____Student Portfolios
_____Student Folders: Type_____
_____Record of Parental Conferences
_____Rollbook

SECTION 3: PREPARATION AND READINESS

_____Textbooks
_____Workbooks

_____Class Lists
_____Seating Chart
_____Record of Student Attendance
_____Students' Cumulative Folders
_____Daily Schedules
_____Audio-Visuals: Type_____
_____Student Notebooks
_____Lesson Planbook
_____Student Information Page (Telephone, Parents)
_____Specialists (Guidance, Nurse, SAC, Lunch, etc.)
_____Packet for Substitute Teacher

SECTION 4: INSTRUCTIONAL PERFORMANCE

_____Posted Instructional Objective/s
_____Test Preparation Strategies
_____Supplementary Materials to Support Objective/s
_____Evidence of Assigned Homework
_____Chalkboard Seatwork/Notes
_____Evidence of Student Grouping
_____Use of Manipulatives/Hands-On Aids by Students

SECTION 5: INTERACTION/CLIMATE

_____Class/School Rules
_____Record of Class Monitors and Tasks
_____Appropriate Seating Arrangement
_____Charts/Posters Relevant to Lesson/Grade/Subject
_____Decorated Bulletin Boards
_____Organized/Aesthetic Classroom
_____Aerated Classroom
_____Clean Classroom
_____Neat Student Desks
_____Organized Learning Centers/Work Areas
_____Parental Involvement Activities

_____

*Use ✓ to indicate that item was observed and/or was made available during the course of the observation/evaluation. Suggestion: Duplicate multiple copies in advance of evaluations.